For Ally, with big, big love

First published in hardback in the United Kingdom by HarperCollins *Children's Books* in 2023
This paperback edition published in 2024
HarperCollins *Children's Books* is a division of HarperCollins*Publishers* Ltd, 1 London Bridge Street, London SE1 9GF
www.harpercollins.co.uk
HarperCollins*Publishers*, Macken House, 39/40 Mayor Street Upper, Dublin 1, D01 C9W8, Ireland

1 3 5 7 9 10 8 6 4 2

Text and illustrations copyright © Rob Biddulph 2023

ISBN: 978-0-00-841344-6

Rob Biddulph asserts the moral right to be identified as the author and illustrator of the work. A CIP catalogue record for this book is available from the British Library. All rights reserved. This book is sold subject to the condition that it shall not, by way of trade or otherwise, be lent, re-sold, hired out or otherwise circulated without the publisher's prior consent in any form, binding or cover other than that in which it is published and without a similar condition including this condition being imposed on the subsequent purchaser.

Printed and bound in India

Five things to find in this book

A pearl in an oyster shell ☐
A tiny alien piloting a submarine ☐
A pirate fish ☐
A message in a bottle ☐
A diamond ring ☐

Written and illustrated by

Rob Biddulph

HarperCollins *Children's Books*

A mulberry sky full of flashes and rumbles.

An ocean alive

His parents they love him, but hope all the same
That one day their son will grow into his name.

"Hey, titchy," taunts Titan. "If I were that small,
I'm not sure I'd feel like a whale at all!"

"In fact, little brother, I think you'd be wise
To make friends with Myrtle. She's much more your size."

So...

they leap...

and they dive...

and they dance...

and they play.

Big fun for small friends in the mouth of the bay.

Meanwhile, plumes of seaweed concealing their bulk,
It's Titan with buddies Colossus and Hulk.

"Just look at those pipsqueaks," he says with a frown.
"Let's get a bit closer, see what's going down."

"Oh, wow," says Colossus, a smile on her chops,
"Gigantic's so good at those flippety flops!"

"Your brother," says Hulk, "is a talent, for sure!
I've not seen a whale do a tailspin before!"

"Nonsense!" says Titan.
"There can't be much to it!

"How hard can it be
if Gigantic can do it?

"I'll show those two shrimps
how a *real* whale can swim.

"And I'll do it BIGGER
and BETTER than him!"

"Wait," says Colossus. "Stay right where you are.
The sea in the bay is too shallow, by far."

Ignoring his friends, the determined young whale
Sets off through the blue with a swish of his tail.

Gigantic looks up as a shadow is cast.
"Be careful..." he warns, as his brother glides past.

So now we arrive at the turn of the tide.
Poor Titan is beached, lying stuck on his side.

"Quickly!" shouts Myrtle,
"This looks like bad news!
SMALL SEA LIFE, ASSEMBLE!
There's no time to lose!"

They come from the coral, the rocks and the caves,
The teenies and tinies that live 'neath the waves.
They dig and they scrape and they scoop and they suck,
All working as one to get Titan unstuck.

"Pull!" bellows Myrtle. "We haven't got long!"

"I'll help!" says Gigantic. "I'm small but I'm strong!"

They heave and they drag and they haul and they strain,
Each one a small link in a much bigger chain.

The little blue whale pulls with all of his might...

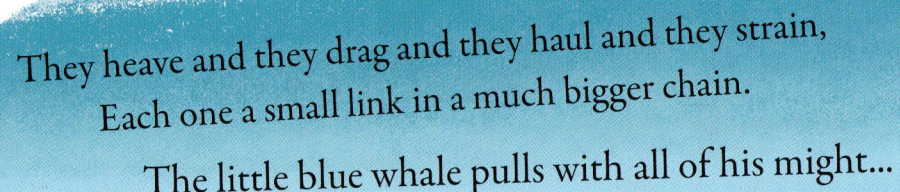

And look! Titan's free!
What a wonderful sight!

Relieved, the huge whale takes his leave of the bay.

Young Titan has learned a hard lesson today.

And here comes Gigantic, a smile on his face...

"Now show us that tailspin, I bet that it's ace!"

"Gigantic," says Titan,
"I've been such a fool.
Enormously dim,
tiny-minded and cruel.

"I was blind to your talents,
but now I can see,
How hugely important
the small things can be.

"From now on I promise
to stop being mean.
I'll be the best brother
the world's ever seen."

An ocean alive,
filled with friends
large AND tiny.

Remember, your height doesn't set you apart.
What matters the most...

...is the size of your heart.